The Islamic Mi

Jamshed

# **Tawakkul**

Cultivating Trust in Allah

The Islamic Mindset Series

www.catalysticcoach.com

Introduction: Understanding Tawakkul

Tawakkul is a deeply spiritual concept in Islam, often translated as "trust in Allah." However, it encompasses much more than that simple phrase. Tawakkul means to rely entirely on Allah for all aspects of life while taking the necessary steps to achieve our goals. It's about understanding that our efforts alone do not determine the outcome—Allah's plan ultimately prevails.

The Qur'an and Sunnah provide numerous examples where believers were tested, yet their unwavering trust in Allah brought them success. Tawakkul is not passive fatalism; rather, it is active reliance on Allah while fulfilling our responsibilities.

In this book, we'll explore how to cultivate and strengthen tawakkul through practical exercises, real-life examples, and an exploration of Islamic teachings. Whether you're going through personal challenges, career obstacles, or spiritual doubts, this book aims to help you anchor your life in trust in Allah.

"Tawakkul isn't about giving up; it's about giving it all to Allah and trusting Him with the outcome." – Jamshed Durrani.

"True peace begins when you realize that your efforts matter, but the results rest in the hands of Allah."

## Chapter 1: The Concept of Tawakkul in Islam

Tawakkul stems from the Arabic word "wakil," meaning a trustee, someone who is in charge of taking care of all matters on behalf of another. In Islam, Allah is the ultimate "Wakil," the one who manages all of our affairs, whether we realize it or not.

The Qur'an emphasizes tawakkul multiple times:

"And whosoever puts his trust in Allah, then He will suffice him." (Qur'an 65:3)

In this chapter, we will explore:

- The linguistic and theological background of tawakkul.
- How tawakkul differs from mere reliance on others or passive acceptance.
- The importance of balancing tawakkul with effort and action, as taught by Prophet Muhammad (PBUH), who said, "Tie your camel and then trust in Allah" (Tirmidhi).

### 1.1 The Linguistic and Theological Background of Tawakkul

The word Tawakkul originates from the Arabic root وكل (wakala), which means to entrust or assign responsibility to another. In an Islamic context, tawakkul signifies placing complete trust in Allah as the sole manager and disposer of all affairs. Theologically, tawakkul reflects a deep acknowledgment of Allah's omnipotence and His ultimate control over every aspect of life.

Allah is often referred to as Al-Wakil (The Trustee), which means the One whom believers trust and rely on. Trusting in Allah means understanding that He knows what is best for us, even when things seem unclear or difficult. This recognition of Allah as our protector and provider is central to the concept of tawakkul.

## 1.2 How Tawakkul Differs from Mere Reliance on Others or Passive Acceptance

One of the key misconceptions about tawakkul is the belief that it equates to simply sitting back and waiting for Allah to handle everything without taking any action. This is not the case. Tawakkul requires active participation from the believer. It means that while you put your trust in Allah for the outcome, you must also make every effort to fulfill your responsibilities.

Tawakkul is distinct from mere reliance on other people or even on one's own abilities. When you trust another person or your own efforts alone, the trust is finite—it is limited by human weaknesses and the unpredictability of life. But when you place your trust in Allah, you rely on His infinite wisdom, mercy, and control.

## 1.3 The Importance of Balancing Tawakkul with Effort and Action

The beauty of tawakkul lies in its balance between effort and trust. It does not encourage passivity or laziness but teaches us to take the necessary steps in achieving our goals while leaving the results to Allah. This concept is perfectly illustrated by the famous hadith of the Prophet Muhammad (PBUH):

"Tie your camel, then put your trust in Allah."
(Tirmidhi)

In this hadith, the Prophet (PBUH) advises a man to secure his camel first—i.e., take practical action to safeguard his belongings—before trusting Allah for the outcome. This shows that tawakkul is a blend of personal effort and spiritual trust. It encourages believers to work hard while keeping faith that Allah will determine what is best.

Key Aspects of Balancing Effort and Tawakkul:

- Personal Responsibility: You must take action and do what is within your control. Whether it's working for a livelihood, seeking medical treatment when ill, or resolving conflicts in relationships, you are required to make every reasonable effort.
- Trust in Allah's Plan: Once you've taken action, you leave the outcome to Allah, trusting that He will provide what is best for you, even if it's not what you expected or hoped for. This removes the anxiety over things you cannot control.
- Gratitude in Both Success and Failure: Tawakkul teaches that even when things don't go according to your plan, there is wisdom in Allah's decree. Whether you succeed or face setbacks, maintaining gratitude and trust in Allah's greater wisdom is essential.

Practical Example: Imagine you are preparing for an important job interview. Tawakkul means that you prepare thoroughly, research the company, practice answering potential questions, and dress appropriately. Once you've done your best, you enter the interview with full reliance on Allah, knowing that He has already decreed what is best for you. If you get the job, you praise Allah for His bounty. If you don't, you remain content, understanding that Allah has something better planned for you.

Exercise 1: Reflecting on Tawakkul in Your Life

- Step 1: Identify three areas of your life where you feel anxious or uncertain (e.g., work, relationships, health).
- Step 2: For each area, write down the actions you are currently taking to improve the situation. Are there any additional steps you can take to fulfill your responsibilities?
- Step 3: After listing your efforts, take a moment to reflect on how much trust you are placing in Allah for the outcome. Are you allowing anxiety or fear to take over, or are you surrendering the result to Allah?

about the "what ifs" and allows you to focus on what is within your control—your effort.

## How Tawakkul Eliminates the Anxiety of "Control" and Overthinking

Many people experience anxiety and stress because they feel a need to control every aspect of their lives. This mindset often leads to overthinking, worry, and frustration when things don't go according to plan. Tawakkul offers a solution to this problem by helping believers realize that control ultimately lies with Allah, not in their hands.

Tawakkul teaches that once you've done your part—once you've put in your best effort—you should stop worrying about the outcome and trust in Allah's wisdom. This eliminates the need to micromanage every detail or obsess over the result.

How Tawakkul Relieves Anxiety:

- Surrendering Control: When you internalize the idea that Allah is in control of the outcomes, you can let go of the fear of failure or disappointment. This doesn't mean giving up, but instead recognizing that whatever happens is part of Allah's plan for you.
- Focusing on What You Can Control: Tawakkul redirects your focus from the things you cannot control (the outcome) to what you can control (your efforts). This shift in mindset reduces overthinking and allows you to concentrate on fulfilling your role in the best possible way.
- Acceptance of Allah's Plan: Even when things don't go your way, tawakkul instills a sense of contentment and peace, knowing that Allah's plan is better than anything you could have imagined for yourself.

By embracing tawakkul, you free yourself from the burden of worrying about the future and instead live in the present moment, trusting that Allah's wisdom is always at work.

Practical Example: The Job Interview Scenario

Let's apply this understanding to a common situation—preparing for a job interview.

1. Taking Action: You prepare for the interview by researching the company, practicing common interview questions, and dressing appropriately. You've done everything within your power to present yourself as the best candidate.
2. Trusting Allah for the Outcome: After the interview, you trust that whatever happens is part of Allah's plan. If you get the job, you thank Allah for the blessing. If you don't, you remain patient and content, trusting that Allah has something better in store for you.
3. Avoiding Anxiety: Because you've placed the outcome in Allah's hands, you don't need to dwell on whether you answered every question perfectly or stress over why you haven't heard back yet. You've done your part, and now you leave the rest to Allah.

By practicing tawakkul, you can approach situations like these with a sense of calm, knowing that your effort matters, but the result is Allah's decree.

Exercise 2: Releasing the Need for Control

- Step 1: Identify a situation in your life where you feel the need to control the outcome (e.g., a project at work, a relationship, or a personal goal).
- Step 2: Write down the actions you have taken or can take to fulfill your responsibilities in that situation.
- Step 3: Reflect on how much you trust Allah with the outcome. Are you overly attached to a specific result, or are you open to Allah's wisdom and plan for you?

- Step 4: Write a short dua asking Allah to guide your efforts and help you release the need to control the outcome. For example:

  "O Allah, I have done my best in this matter. I trust in Your wisdom, and I leave the outcome in Your hands. Grant me peace of mind and contentment with whatever You have decreed."

- Step 5: Every time you feel anxiety or stress over the outcome, repeat this dua and remind yourself that the result is from Allah, not from your efforts alone.

This exercise will help you practice tawakkul in a real-life situation, teaching you to balance effort with trust in Allah and freeing you from the anxiety of needing to control every detail.

Conclusion

In this chapter, we have explored the balance between taking action and trusting in Allah. Tawakkul does not mean avoiding responsibility or relying solely on prayer; it is about exerting effort while fully trusting that the outcome is in Allah's hands. This understanding helps eliminate the anxiety of control and teaches us to focus on what we can do while leaving the results to Allah, who knows what is best for us.

By embracing this mindset, we can approach life's challenges with confidence, calmness, and peace, knowing that Allah will provide us with what we need when we need it.

"Our plans may fail, but Allah's plan is always perfect. Trusting in Him gives us the strength to keep going."

Chapter 3: The Role of Patience in Tawakkul

Tawakkul is deeply intertwined with patience (sabr). Trusting in Allah requires waiting for the results of your efforts with a heart full of faith. When you have done all that you can, patience helps to maintain that trust without becoming frustrated or anxious.

This chapter will cover:

- The Qur'anic connection between sabr and tawakkul.
- The different levels of patience and how they relate to faith.
- Why trusting Allah during trials strengthens your spiritual resilience.

3.1 The Qur'anic Connection Between Sabr and Tawakkul

In the Qur'an, the concepts of sabr (patience) and tawakkul (trust in Allah) are frequently mentioned together, illustrating their deep connection. Both qualities are essential for developing spiritual resilience, especially during times of hardship and trials. The Qur'an states:

"And be patient. Surely, Allah is with those who are patient."
(Qur'an 8:46)

In another verse, Allah connects patience with trust:

"So be patient. Indeed, the promise of Allah is truth. And let not those who have no certainty of faith discourage you from your resolve."
(Qur'an 30:60)

These verses highlight that those who are patient are not only enduring but also relying on Allah with full faith in His wisdom. The Qur'an teaches that while patience helps you persevere through challenges, tawakkul strengthens your heart with trust in Allah's ultimate plan, allowing you to find comfort in knowing that He is in control of all outcomes.

3.2 The Different Levels of Patience and Their Relation to Faith

Sabr in Islam is not just about waiting for a difficulty to pass; it is an active form of endurance that reflects the strength of one's faith. There are different levels of patience that every believer can cultivate, and each level reflects a deeper connection to Allah.

1. Patience in Obeying Allah: This level of patience involves remaining steadfast in acts of worship, even when it is difficult. Whether it's praying regularly, fasting during Ramadan, or giving charity, obedience requires continuous effort and perseverance. The stronger a person's faith, the more willing they are to push through any obstacles to stay connected to Allah.
2. Patience in Refraining from Sin: Another form of patience is the ability to resist temptation and avoid sinful behavior. It takes resilience to fight against the desires of the nafs (ego) and stay committed to the boundaries set by Allah. This kind of patience reflects a high level of self-control and trust that Allah will provide something better than what is temporarily desired.
3. Patience in Facing Trials and Hardships: This is the most commonly understood form of sabr—being patient during difficulties, such as illness, loss, or financial struggles. True faith is demonstrated when a believer faces hardship without complaining, maintaining trust in Allah's plan. Those who exhibit this level of patience have internalized the belief that Allah is always with them, and that every trial serves a purpose.

Each of these levels of patience reflects a different aspect of the believer's relationship with Allah. The deeper the faith, the stronger the believer's patience in all aspects of life.

3.3 Why Trusting Allah During Trials Strengthens Your Spiritual Resilience

One of the most profound ways to strengthen your spiritual resilience is by combining sabr with tawakkul during times of difficulty. When you trust Allah through your trials, you are able to endure hardship with a sense of peace and surrender, knowing that Allah's wisdom surpasses your understanding.

Trusting Allah in difficult moments shifts your mindset from focusing on the pain to recognizing that every trial carries a divine purpose. The Prophet Muhammad (PBUH) said:

"Wondrous is the affair of the believer, for there is good for him in every matter, and this is not the case with anyone except the believer. If he is happy, then he thanks Allah, and thus there is good for him. And if he is harmed, then he shows patience, and thus there is good for him."
(Sahih Muslim)

This hadith emphasizes that for a believer, whether in ease or hardship, there is always an opportunity to draw closer to Allah. By trusting Allah during a trial, you shift from being consumed by the challenge to seeing it as an opportunity for growth and spiritual elevation.

The Benefits of Combining Sabr and Tawakkul:

- Emotional Resilience: Trusting Allah reduces the anxiety and fear that often accompany hardships. When you realize that Allah is in control, you are better able to accept what is happening with peace, knowing that every hardship will eventually pass.
- Strengthening Iman (Faith): Every time you practice sabr and tawakkul during a difficult moment, your faith deepens. You begin to recognize that no challenge is too great when Allah is by your side, and this strengthens your connection to Him.
- Spiritual Growth: Trials are often a means for purification and growth. By trusting Allah, you allow yourself to emerge from a hardship with a stronger, more resilient spirit.

Table of Contents

1. Introduction: Understanding Tawakkul
2. Chapter 1: The Concept of Tawakkul in Islam
3. Chapter 2: The Balance Between Effort and Tawakkul
4. Chapter 3: The Role of Patience in Tawakkul
5. Chapter 4: How Tawakkul Strengthens Faith and Reduces Anxiety
6. Chapter 5: Practical Steps to Develop Tawakkul in Daily Life
7. Chapter 6: Stories of Tawakkul from the Prophets
8. Chapter 7: How to Teach Tawakkul to Children
9. Chapter 8: Exercises to Strengthen Your Trust in Allah
10. Chapter 9: Overcoming Doubts and Challenges with Tawakkul
11. Conclusion: Living a Life Anchored in Trust

**Note from the Author:** The Islamic Mindset Series – Tawakkul: Cultivating Trust in Allah

Bismillah ar-Rahman ar-Rahim (In the name of Allah, the Most Gracious, the Most Merciful)

Dear Reader,

It is with immense gratitude that I present to you this volume of The Islamic Mindset Series, focusing on one of the most profound concepts in Islam—Tawakkul. In this fast-paced and unpredictable world, the need to trust in Allah's plan has never been more essential. Tawakkul is the bridge between our efforts and Allah's divine wisdom, offering us peace and reassurance in the face of life's uncertainties.

Throughout this book, we explore how Tawakkul empowers us to live with a deep sense of reliance on Allah while encouraging proactive effort in our daily lives. This balance of trust and action is at the heart of our faith, as exemplified by the Prophet Muhammad's (PBUH) teachings.

The Islamic Mindset Series is designed to help you cultivate spiritual resilience and mental clarity by incorporating key Islamic principles into your mindset. This volume on Tawakkul, in particular, aims to provide practical insights, heart-touching stories, and exercises that will strengthen your trust in Allah, helping you navigate life's trials with grace and confidence.

It is my sincere hope that this book will inspire you to live with a heart anchored in Tawakkul, trusting in Allah's perfect plan while actively striving for personal and spiritual excellence.

May Allah (SWT) guide you on your journey and bless you with unwavering faith.

Warm regards,
Jamshed Durrani

- Step 4: Write a short dua for each situation, asking Allah to guide your efforts and grant you success, while also trusting in His wisdom no matter the outcome.

This exercise will help you evaluate your balance between effort and trust, encouraging you to adopt a mindset of active tawakkul.

By understanding the linguistic and theological roots of tawakkul, distinguishing it from passive acceptance, and learning how to balance personal effort with spiritual reliance, you begin your journey toward a more trusting, faithful, and empowered way of living.

Tawakkul transforms fear into faith, stress into serenity, and uncertainty into trust."
Chapter 2: The Balance Between Effort and Tawakkul

One of the misconceptions about tawakkul is that it negates the need for personal effort. Islam teaches a balance between exerting effort and trusting in Allah for the results. Prophet Muhammad (PBUH) exemplified this in his own life—he planned and strategized in battles, but his trust was in Allah.

Key points covered in this chapter include:

- The concept of asababu minallah (means are from Allah).
- Understanding that your responsibility is to take action, but the result is from Allah alone.
- How tawakkul eliminates the anxiety of "control" and overthinking, allowing you to focus on fulfilling your role in the best possible way.

The Concept of Asababu Minallah (Means Are from Allah)

One of the foundational concepts in tawakkul is asababu minallah—the idea that the means by which we achieve things come from Allah. This means that while we are responsible for working toward our goals, the resources, abilities, and opportunities we utilize to get there are all part of Allah's provision.

For example, when you strive to earn a livelihood, your skills, job opportunities, and even the energy to work are all means that Allah has granted you. You are expected to use these means to fulfill your responsibilities, but you must always remember that they ultimately originate from Allah, not from your own doing alone.

Understanding asababu minallah allows you to see the hand of Allah in every success and failure, knowing that He alone controls the means and the ends.

Your Responsibility to Take Action, But the Result Is from Allah Alone

Islam teaches that human beings are accountable for their actions, but the results of those actions are entirely in the hands of Allah. The Qur'an says:

"And that there is not for man except that [good] for which he strives, and that his effort is going to be seen—then he will be recompensed for it with the fullest recompense."
(Qur'an 53:39-41)

This verse emphasizes the importance of striving, of making an effort, while recognizing that the ultimate outcome is in Allah's hands. You are responsible for doing your best, but the outcome is part of Allah's divine plan. Whether you succeed, fail, or face unexpected results, it is important to trust that Allah knows what is best for you.

This teaches us two important lessons:

1. Hard Work Is Essential: You are obligated to work hard and strive for excellence in everything you do. This is part of being a responsible and proactive Muslim.
2. Outcome Is Beyond Your Control: While you work hard, you must not become attached to the outcome, as the result is from Allah alone. This frees you from the constant worry

- Step 1: Identify a situation in your life that is causing you stress or anxiety (e.g., financial troubles, relationship problems, health concerns).
- Step 2: Write down the practical steps you can take to address the situation. What actions are within your control?
- Step 3: Reflect on how you can place trust in Allah for the outcome. Make a dua asking Allah to guide you in this situation and help you trust His plan.
- Step 4: Whenever anxiety or fear arises, remind yourself that Allah is in control. Repeat the following verse:

  "Hasbunallahu wa ni'mal wakeel" (Allah is sufficient for us, and He is the best disposer of affairs).

- Step 5: Review how this practice affects your level of anxiety over the course of the week. Do you feel more at peace knowing that Allah is guiding the outcome?

## Conclusion

In this chapter, we explored how tawakkul serves as both a source of inner peace and a powerful tool for reducing anxiety. By trusting in Allah's wisdom and control, we release ourselves from the burden of overthinking and worrying about what the future holds. Tawakkul strengthens our faith by deepening our reliance on Allah and nurturing our patience during trials. Ultimately, tawakkul helps us live more contentedly, knowing that Allah's plan is always for our benefit.

As you continue to practice tawakkul, you will find that your anxieties lessen and your faith strengthens, enabling you to navigate life's challenges with resilience, peace, and a deeper trust in Allah's infinite wisdom.

deeper reliance on Allah and strengthens our faith that everything happens for a reason.
- Gratitude for Allah's Mercy: As we experience the fruits of tawakkul—whether through answered prayers, unexpected blessings, or personal growth during hardship—we develop a sense of gratitude. Gratitude, in turn, nurtures our faith, as we come to appreciate Allah's mercy and guidance in every situation.

4.4 Practical Example: Trusting Allah in Uncertainty

Imagine you are going through a financial struggle, unsure of how you will pay your bills or provide for your family. It's natural to feel anxious in this situation. However, instead of allowing worry to overwhelm you, you practice tawakkul by taking the following steps:

1. Taking Action: You do your part by actively seeking job opportunities, applying for financial assistance, or finding ways to reduce expenses. This shows your willingness to put in the effort.
2. Trusting Allah: After you've done what you can, you place the matter in Allah's hands, trusting that He will provide for you, whether through an unexpected job offer, a helping hand from a friend, or another avenue.
3. Letting Go of Worry: Rather than obsessing over the situation, you remember that Allah is Al-Razzaq (The Provider) and trust that He will find a way to relieve your financial burden. You remain calm, knowing that Allah will take care of your needs in His own way.

By practicing tawakkul in this way, you strengthen your faith and reduce the anxiety that comes with uncertainty.

Exercise 4: Cultivating Tawakkul to Reduce Anxiety

"Tawakkul teaches us that the real power lies not in control, but in submission to Allah's wisdom."

## Chapter 5: Practical Steps to Develop Tawakkul in Daily Life

Tawakkul isn't something that happens overnight. Like any spiritual practice, it requires regular attention and effort. This chapter provides practical tips and strategies to incorporate tawakkul into your daily life, including:

- Daily dua and remembrance (dhikr) that emphasizes trust in Allah.
- Building a routine that includes moments of reflection on Allah's control and wisdom.
- Setting realistic expectations for yourself and accepting the outcome, even if it's not what you wanted.

Tawakkul, or placing trust in Allah, is not just a belief but a practice that can be cultivated through conscious effort in everyday life. By actively implementing tawakkul in daily situations, you strengthen your faith and develop a mindset of trust, reliance, and peace. Here are practical steps to help you develop tawakkul in your daily life:

### 1. Start with Niyyah (Intention)

Everything in Islam begins with intention. To cultivate tawakkul, make a sincere intention to place your trust in Allah in every aspect of your life. Before starting any task—whether it's related to work, family, or personal goals—pause and remind yourself that you are doing it for the sake of Allah and that the outcome is ultimately in His hands.

- Example: Before starting your day or a specific task, make dua and say, "O Allah, I place my trust in You for the success of this task and whatever You decree as best for me."

### 2. Take Action and Make Effort

Tawakkul is not about passively waiting for things to happen; it involves taking action while trusting that Allah will guide the outcome. The Prophet Muhammad (PBUH) famously said, "Tie your camel and then trust in Allah." (Tirmidhi). This hadith highlights the balance between effort and trust in Allah.

- Example: If you are applying for a job, take proactive steps like updating your resume, applying to different positions, and preparing for interviews. Once you've done your part, place your trust in Allah for the result.

3. Practice Gratitude for the Present

Tawakkul also involves being content and grateful for your current situation. Often, anxiety arises from focusing too much on future outcomes. By practicing gratitude for the present, you remind yourself of Allah's ongoing blessings and foster a mindset of trust.

- Example: Start a daily gratitude journal. Each day, write down three things you are grateful for, and reflect on how Allah has provided for you in the past.

4. Incorporate Dhikr (Remembrance of Allah)

Dhikr is a powerful tool for strengthening tawakkul. By consistently remembering Allah throughout the day, you keep your heart connected to Him and reaffirm your trust in His wisdom and plan. Dhikr helps to calm anxiety and refocus your mind on Allah's control over all matters.

- Example: Recite "Hasbunallahu wa ni'mal wakeel" (Allah is sufficient for us, and He is the best disposer of affairs) regularly, especially when feeling stressed or overwhelmed. Another recommended dhikr is "La hawla wa la quwwata illa billah" (There is no power or strength except with Allah).

5. Seek Knowledge About Tawakkul

One way to deepen your trust in Allah is to continuously seek knowledge about tawakkul from the Qur'an and the life of the

Prophet (PBUH). Understanding how tawakkul is emphasized in Islamic teachings and reflecting on examples from the Prophets will strengthen your conviction.

- Example: Study verses from the Qur'an that emphasize tawakkul, such as Surah At-Tawbah (9:51) and Surah Al-Imran (3:159). Read stories of the Prophets like Ibrahim (AS) and Musa (AS), who exemplified complete trust in Allah in the most challenging circumstances.

6. Let Go of the Need to Control

A major aspect of developing tawakkul is learning to let go of the need to control every detail of your life. While planning and effort are necessary, excessive worrying and trying to control outcomes leads to stress and anxiety. Instead, remind yourself that once you've done your part, the result is in Allah's hands.

- Example: If you're planning a big event or making an important decision, avoid overthinking every possible outcome. Instead, after taking the necessary steps, make dua for Allah to guide you to what is best and let go of the need to control the specifics.

7. Make Dua for Tawakkul

Ask Allah to help you develop tawakkul and place more trust in Him. Dua is a powerful way to connect with Allah and seek His assistance in becoming more reliant on Him. Regularly asking for His guidance in matters of trust and patience will help strengthen your tawakkul over time.

- Example: A suggested dua for tawakkul is:
  "O Allah, grant me the strength to trust in Your plan, the patience to endure what I do not understand, and the wisdom to leave my affairs in Your hands."

8. Reflect on Past Experiences

Look back on past situations where you placed your trust in Allah and how things worked out for the best, even if they didn't go as you initially planned. Reflecting on Allah's wisdom in past events can remind you of His perfect plan and increase your reliance on Him for future matters.

- Example: Write down past challenges that you've faced and how Allah provided a way out or a better outcome than you expected. Use these reflections as reminders when you are struggling to trust in Allah during a current difficulty.

9. Be Patient with the Process

Developing tawakkul takes time, patience, and practice. It is a journey of constantly reminding yourself to trust in Allah, especially during difficult times. Remember that setbacks are part of life and that every challenge is an opportunity to strengthen your trust in Allah.

- Example: When faced with a delay or setback, remind yourself that Allah's timing is perfect. Practice saying "InshaAllah" (if Allah wills) and focus on doing your best, knowing that Allah is guiding you toward what is best.

10. Surround Yourself with People Who Encourage Tawakkul

Being around people who remind you to trust in Allah will help you strengthen your own tawakkul. Seek out companions who uplift your faith, encourage patience, and provide perspective during times of stress.

- Example: Join an Islamic study group or attend classes that focus on the development of trust and reliance on Allah. Engage in conversations with friends and family about how tawakkul has positively impacted their lives, and learn from their experiences.

Exercise 3: Building Patience and Trust in Daily Life

- Step 1: Reflect on a recent challenge you faced (e.g., financial difficulty, family conflict, or health issue). How did you respond to this challenge? Were you able to practice patience, or did you feel anxious or frustrated?
- Step 2: Write down the actions you took to address the challenge. Did you take practical steps, and did you combine those efforts with trust in Allah for the outcome?
- Step 3: Reflect on how you can increase both patience and trust in your daily life. What small actions can you take to practice more sabr and tawakkul when faced with minor or major difficulties?
- Step 4: Make a dua asking Allah for strength in patience and greater trust in His wisdom. For example:

> "O Allah, grant me patience in times of difficulty and bless me with the ability to trust in Your plan, knowing that You are the best disposer of all affairs. Ameen."

Conclusion

In this chapter, we explored the strong connection between sabr (patience) and tawakkul (trust in Allah), as well as the different levels of patience that a believer must cultivate throughout life. Trusting Allah during trials not only helps you navigate through hardship with grace but also strengthens your faith and spiritual resilience. The next time you face a challenge, remember that by practicing patience and trusting in Allah's wisdom, you are aligning yourself with the essence of what it means to be a true believer.

"Faith is not just believing in Allah, but trusting Him in every detail of our lives."

## Chapter 4: How Tawakkul Strengthens Faith and Reduces Anxiety

Tawakkul, the act of placing complete trust in Allah, serves as a powerful tool for strengthening faith and alleviating anxiety. In this chapter, we will explore how tawakkul, when properly understood and practiced, helps cultivate inner peace, reduce stress, and bring about a deeper, more resilient connection to Allah. We will also examine the psychological benefits of trusting in Allah and how it transforms everyday challenges into opportunities for spiritual growth.

### 4.1 Tawakkul as a Source of Inner Peace

The modern world is full of stressors—financial pressures, relationship issues, health concerns, and uncertainty about the future. These challenges often lead to feelings of anxiety and overwhelm. However, the Islamic concept of tawakkul offers a pathway to inner peace. By trusting in Allah, we acknowledge that while we must do our best in every situation, the ultimate control over our lives rests with Him.

The Qur'an says:

"And whosoever fears Allah and keeps his duty to Him, He will make a way for him to get out (from every difficulty). And He will provide him from (sources) he never could imagine. And whosoever puts his trust in Allah, then He will suffice him."
(Qur'an 65:2-3)

This verse encapsulates the essence of tawakkul—when we place our trust in Allah, He will provide us with relief from our difficulties in ways we could never have anticipated. This realization brings profound peace of mind. When we understand that Allah is the ultimate Provider and Planner, we can let go of excessive worry about the future, knowing that He will always guide us to what is best for us.

How Tawakkul Brings Inner Peace:

- Surrendering to Allah's Will: Tawakkul helps us accept that we are not in control of every outcome, freeing us from the need to micromanage every detail of our lives.
- Belief in Allah's Plan: Trusting that Allah's plan is always for our ultimate good—even when we don't understand it—brings reassurance and calm during times of uncertainty.
- Focus on the Present: Tawakkul shifts our focus from worrying about future outcomes to living in the present moment, trusting that Allah is guiding us along the best path.

4.2 The Role of Tawakkul in Reducing Anxiety and Stress

Anxiety often stems from fear of the unknown and an overwhelming desire to control every aspect of life. Tawakkul directly addresses these sources of anxiety by teaching us to place our trust in Allah for the outcomes of our efforts. While we are responsible for taking action, tawakkul teaches us to let go of the need for control over the results.

The Prophet Muhammad (PBUH) said:

"If you were to rely upon Allah with the reliance He is due, you would be given provision like the birds: they go out in the morning hungry and return full."
(Tirmidhi)

This hadith beautifully illustrates the essence of tawakkul. Just as birds leave their nests each morning without knowing where they will find food, we too must work toward our goals without fear, knowing that Allah will provide for us. The birds do not worry about whether they will find sustenance—they do their part by searching, and Allah provides. This mindset reduces anxiety and allows us to move through life with confidence and trust in Allah's plan.

How Tawakkul Reduces Anxiety:

- **Letting Go of the Fear of Failure:** Anxiety often arises from the fear of failing or not achieving a desired outcome. Tawakkul teaches that success is not solely in our hands but in Allah's control. Once we have done our part, we can trust that the result, whether success or setback, is what is best for us.
- **Trust in Allah's Wisdom:** Tawakkul allows us to trust that even when things don't go as planned, Allah's wisdom is at work. This trust helps alleviate the fear of the unknown and brings a sense of calm during uncertainty.
- **Freedom from Overthinking:** Overthinking can be a significant source of stress. Tawakkul helps us release the need to overanalyze every situation. Instead of constantly worrying about "what if," we place the outcome in Allah's hands, allowing ourselves to relax and focus on the present.

## 4.3 Strengthening Faith Through Tawakkul

Tawakkul not only helps reduce anxiety, but it also strengthens faith. When we trust in Allah, we develop a deeper connection with Him, knowing that He is always with us and looking after our best interests. Tawakkul is an active demonstration of our belief in Allah's omnipotence and mercy.

Each time we practice tawakkul, we are reaffirming our trust in Allah's plan, even when things seem difficult or unclear. This deepens our iman (faith), as we realize that no situation is beyond Allah's control and that He is always guiding us through life's trials.

How Tawakkul Strengthens Faith:

- **Seeing Allah's Hand in Every Situation:** When we trust Allah fully, we start to recognize His presence and help in every aspect of our lives, even in seemingly small or mundane matters. This awareness strengthens our belief in Allah's constant care.
- **Patience and Perseverance:** Tawakkul teaches patience. When we face delays or setbacks, rather than losing hope, we trust that Allah's timing is perfect. This patience fosters a

Exercise 5: Developing Tawakkul in Your Daily Life

1. Reflect on a Current Challenge: Identify a current challenge or situation where you are feeling anxious or stressed. Write it down and reflect on what actions are within your control.
2. Take Action: Write down three steps you can take to address the situation. Once you've taken those steps, consciously leave the rest in Allah's hands.
3. Trust and Let Go: Whenever feelings of anxiety or control resurface, recite the dhikr "Hasbunallahu wa ni'mal wakeel" and remind yourself that Allah's wisdom is greater than yours.
4. Daily Gratitude: Write down one thing you are grateful for each day that reflects how Allah has provided for you in the past. Use this as a reminder of His continued care in your life.
5. Make Dua: At the end of each day, make dua asking Allah to help you place your trust in Him fully and guide you to what is best.


Conclusion

Developing tawakkul is a lifelong journey that requires continuous practice and reflection. By actively trusting Allah in your daily life, you release the burden of anxiety, increase your patience, and grow closer to Him. The more you practice placing your reliance on Allah, the more peaceful and resilient you will become, knowing that your life is always in the care of the One who knows what is best for you. Through daily intentions, actions, and gratitude, tawakkul becomes not just a belief but a way of life.

"When we anchor our hearts in Tawakkul, we're not shaken by the storms of life because we know Allah is in control."

## Chapter 6: Stories of Tawakkul from the Prophets

The Prophets of Islam are the greatest examples of complete trust and reliance on Allah. Their lives are filled with trials and challenges, yet they consistently demonstrated unwavering faith in Allah's plan. In this chapter, we will explore stories of tawakkul (trust in Allah) from the lives of some of the Prophets. These stories serve as powerful lessons, showing how tawakkul leads to victory, relief, and a deeper connection with Allah, even in the most difficult situations.

### 6.1 The Story of Prophet Ibrahim (AS): Trusting Allah in the Fire

One of the most profound examples of tawakkul comes from the life of Prophet Ibrahim (AS). His trust in Allah was tested in various ways, but the most well-known story is when he was thrown into a fire by his people for refusing to worship idols.

Ibrahim (AS) had challenged the idol worshippers of his time, explaining to them that only Allah deserves to be worshipped. Enraged by his message, the people decided to punish him by throwing him into a massive fire. As the fire was being prepared, Ibrahim (AS) remained calm and placed his trust in Allah. He said:

"Sufficient for us is Allah, and He is the best disposer of affairs." (Surah Al-Imran 3:173)

When Ibrahim (AS) was thrown into the fire, Allah commanded the fire to be cool and peaceful for him. Instead of harming him, the fire became a place of comfort. This miraculous event demonstrated the power of tawakkul—when a believer places their complete trust in Allah, He will protect and provide for them in ways beyond human understanding.

Lesson: The story of Prophet Ibrahim (AS) teaches us that even in the face of extreme danger, when the situation seems hopeless, tawakkul can lead to miracles. Trusting Allah means believing that He will protect you, even when the world is against you.

## 6.2 The Story of Prophet Musa (AS): Trusting Allah at the Red Sea

Prophet Musa (AS) also exemplified tawakkul in a moment of great peril. After liberating the Israelites from the oppression of Pharaoh, Musa (AS) and his people found themselves trapped between the Red Sea and Pharaoh's approaching army. The situation seemed dire—there was no way forward, and certain destruction seemed imminent.

Despite the panic of the people, Musa (AS) remained firm in his trust in Allah. He reassured his followers:

"Indeed, my Lord is with me; He will guide me."
(Surah Ash-Shu'ara 26:62)

In that moment of complete reliance on Allah, the sea was miraculously parted, allowing Musa (AS) and the Israelites to cross safely. When Pharaoh and his army followed, the sea closed upon them, leading to their destruction.

Lesson: Musa's (AS) story teaches us that even in the most impossible situations, where escape or success seems unlikely, tawakkul opens the doors to Allah's help. It reminds us that Allah can provide a way out of any difficulty, as long as we trust in Him fully.

## 6.3 The Story of Prophet Yunus (AS): Trusting Allah in the Belly of the Whale

Prophet Yunus (AS) provides another powerful example of tawakkul. After preaching to his people and feeling frustrated by their rejection of his message, Yunus (AS) left his town without Allah's permission. Soon after, he was swallowed by a great whale while on a ship in the middle of the sea.

In the belly of the whale, in the depths of the ocean, Yunus (AS) realized his mistake and turned to Allah in sincere repentance and trust. He called out:

"There is no deity except You; exalted are You. Indeed, I have been of the wrongdoers."
(Surah Al-Anbiya 21:87)

Yunus (AS) placed his complete trust in Allah's mercy, and after three days, Allah commanded the whale to release him onto the shore. Yunus (AS) was saved, and he returned to his people with renewed faith and determination.

Lesson: The story of Yunus (AS) teaches us that even when we make mistakes or find ourselves in seemingly hopeless situations, tawakkul allows us to return to Allah and seek His forgiveness. Trusting in Allah's mercy and wisdom can lead to redemption and salvation, no matter how difficult the circumstances.

6.4 The Story of Prophet Muhammad (PBUH): Trusting Allah During the Hijrah

The Prophet Muhammad (PBUH) showed immense trust in Allah throughout his life, but one of the most remarkable examples of tawakkul is during the Hijrah (migration) from Mecca to Medina. When the Quraysh plotted to kill him, the Prophet (PBUH) and his companion, Abu Bakr (RA), sought refuge in a cave on the outskirts of Mecca.

As the Quraysh pursued them, they came close to discovering the Prophet's hiding place. Abu Bakr (RA) became anxious, fearing that they would be found. However, the Prophet (PBUH) reassured him, saying:

"Do not grieve; indeed, Allah is with us."
(Surah At-Tawbah 9:40)

Despite the danger, the Prophet (PBUH) placed his complete trust in Allah, and as a result, Allah protected them. The Quraysh, though they came close, did not find the cave, and the Prophet (PBUH) safely made his way to Medina.

Lesson: The Hijrah story teaches us that when we trust in Allah, He is always with us, protecting and guiding us through life's challenges. Tawakkul brings a sense of calm and confidence, even in the face of imminent danger or difficulty.

6.5 The Story of Hajar: Trusting Allah in the Desert

Hajar, the wife of Prophet Ibrahim (AS), is a symbol of immense tawakkul. After Ibrahim (AS) left her and their infant son, Ismail (AS), in the barren desert of Mecca, she was left alone with no water or food. Despite her dire situation, Hajar trusted in Allah's plan and continued to search for water, running between the hills of Safa and Marwa.

After her relentless effort, Allah rewarded her trust and perseverance by miraculously providing the spring of Zamzam, which continues to flow to this day.

Lesson: Hajar's story shows us that tawakkul must be paired with effort. She didn't sit passively waiting for help; she actively sought water while trusting Allah's plan. Tawakkul teaches us to work hard and trust that Allah will provide, even when the situation seems impossible.


Exercise: Reflecting on the Prophets' Tawakkul

1. Choose a Story: Select one of the stories from this chapter that resonates with your current situation. Are you facing a difficulty similar to Prophet Ibrahim (AS) or Prophet Musa (AS)?
2. Reflect on Tawakkul: Write down how the Prophet or person in the story demonstrated tawakkul in the face of adversity. What actions did they take, and how did they place their trust in Allah?

3. Apply It to Your Life: Consider how you can apply the lessons of tawakkul from the story to your own life. Are there steps you can take to trust Allah more deeply in your current challenges?
4. Make Dua: Ask Allah to help you develop tawakkul like the Prophets, who trusted Him in every situation. Make a personal dua that Allah grants you strength, patience, and trust in His plan.

Conclusion

The stories of tawakkul from the lives of the Prophets are not just historical accounts; they are timeless lessons for every believer. These stories remind us that no matter how difficult our circumstances, placing our complete trust in Allah will always lead to relief and victory. By reflecting on these stories and applying their lessons to our own lives, we can strengthen our faith, deepen our reliance on Allah, and navigate life's challenges with confidence and peace.

"Effort is our duty, but the outcome is always Allah's gift to us. Trust that whatever He wills is for our ultimate good."

## Chapter 7: How to Teach Tawakkul to Children

Teaching tawakkul to children from an early age can help build a foundation of trust and reliance on Allah as they grow. By introducing this concept in an age-appropriate way, you nurture their spiritual development and help them understand that they are not alone in the challenges they face. In this chapter, we will explore various methods to explain and instill tawakkul in children, including activities, stories, and practices that encourage trust in Allah.

### 2.1 Age-Appropriate Ways to Explain Tawakkul

When introducing children to the concept of tawakkul, it's essential to keep explanations simple and relatable. Here are some approaches for different age groups:

For Toddlers and Preschoolers (Ages 3-6): At this age, children are just beginning to understand basic concepts about Allah and the world around them. Use simple language to explain that Allah is always there to help and protect them.

- Example Explanation: "Tawakkul means that we do our best, and then we trust that Allah will take care of the rest. Allah loves us and always knows what's best for us."
- Relatable Metaphor: Compare tawakkul to holding their parent's hand when crossing the street. Just as they trust their parent to guide them, they should trust Allah to guide them through life.

For Young Children (Ages 7-10): Children in this age group can begin to understand cause and effect, as well as the importance of effort. You can introduce the idea that while we work hard, the results are always in Allah's hands.

- Example Explanation: "Tawakkul means we work hard and do our best, but we know that Allah is the One who decides what happens in the end. Just like when you study for a test, you do your best, and then you trust that Allah will help you with the results."
- Metaphor: Use the metaphor of planting seeds. "When you plant a seed, you take care of it by watering it and giving it sunlight, but only Allah can make it grow."

For Pre-teens and Teens (Ages 11 and Up): Older children can grasp more complex ideas about faith, effort, and the unseen nature of Allah's plan. You can introduce the concept of balancing effort and trust, using examples from their daily lives.

- Example Explanation: "Tawakkul is like preparing for something important—whether it's a test, a competition, or a challenge. You prepare and do your part, but you don't worry about the result, because you know that Allah is in control. Whatever happens, it's part of His wisdom, and it's always for your benefit."
- Metaphor: Explain tawakkul using the metaphor of a ship. "Imagine you're sailing a ship. You steer it, set the sails, and guide it, but you trust Allah to bring the wind and waves to take you to where He knows is best."

2.2 Activities and Stories to Instill Trust in Allah

Children learn best through engaging activities and relatable stories. By integrating tawakkul into their everyday lives, you help them build a lasting connection with this concept.

1. Storytelling: Stories are powerful tools to teach children about important values. Here are two examples of stories that illustrate tawakkul in action:

- The Story of Prophet Ibrahim (AS) in the Fire: Share the story of how Prophet Ibrahim (AS) trusted Allah when his people threw him into the fire. Explain how, because of his

trust, Allah protected him, and the fire became cool and peaceful for him.
- The Story of Hajar's Search for Water: Tell the story of Hajar, who ran between the hills of Safa and Marwa searching for water for her baby Ismail. Explain how she trusted that Allah would help her, and as a result of her effort and tawakkul, the Zamzam well was provided.

After telling these stories, ask the children what they learned about trusting Allah. Encourage them to share how they might apply tawakkul in their own lives.

2. Role-Playing: Role-playing scenarios can help children practice tawakkul. Create simple situations where they can apply the concept of trust in Allah.

- Example Activity: Set up a challenge for the children, like balancing a stack of blocks. Once they've completed the task, explain that just like they worked hard to balance the blocks, they also trust that Allah will guide and help them in other challenges, whether it's in school, friendships, or activities.

3. Gratitude Journals: Encourage children to keep a gratitude journal where they list things they are thankful for. This helps them recognize Allah's blessings and see how He provides for them.

- Exercise: Each night, ask children to write down or draw one thing they worked hard on and how they trusted Allah for the outcome. This reinforces the practice of tawakkul and gratitude in their daily lives.

4. Dua (Supplication) Time: Teach children the importance of making dua and placing their trust in Allah. After completing an activity or challenge, encourage them to make dua, asking Allah for help and expressing their trust in His plan.

- Simple Dua Example: "O Allah, I trust You to help me with this, and I know You always know what is best for me."

## 2.3 Encouraging Children to See the Connection Between Their Efforts and Allah's Plan

It is crucial to help children understand the balance between their own efforts and Allah's plan. Children should realize that while they are responsible for doing their best, the results are always in Allah's hands, and He knows what is best for them.

Here's how you can encourage this understanding:

1. Emphasize Effort Before Outcome: When children are working on something—whether it's a homework assignment, a game, or a chore—remind them that their effort is important, but the result is up to Allah.

- Example: "You did your best on this test, and now we trust that Allah will take care of the rest. No matter what score you get, Allah knows what's best for you."

2. Focus on the Journey, Not Just the Destination: Help children appreciate the process of working hard, even if the outcome is not exactly what they expected. This builds resilience and patience, two key components of tawakkul.

- Example: If a child doesn't win a competition or get the result they wanted, remind them that Allah's plan may have something even better for them in the future, and their effort will never go to waste.

3. Teach Through Nature: Use examples from nature to show children how effort and trust in Allah work together. For instance, explain how birds search for food each day, but ultimately, it's Allah who provides for them.

- Activity: Go on a nature walk and point out how plants grow, animals find food, and the sun rises and sets—all signs of Allah's care and control over the world. Relate this to how Allah takes care of us when we trust Him.

Exercise 1: Trust in Action

Goal: Teach children to apply tawakkul in everyday situations.

1. Choose a Task: Ask your child to pick a small task they need to complete, like cleaning their room, finishing homework, or trying something new.
2. Make an Intention: Help them make the intention that they will do their best for the sake of Allah.
3. Dua for Help: Before starting the task, guide them in making a short dua, asking Allah to help them succeed and trusting Him for the result.
4. Reflect: After completing the task, ask them how it felt to trust in Allah. Did they feel more relaxed knowing Allah was with them?
5. Gratitude: Encourage them to thank Allah, regardless of the outcome, acknowledging that He knows what is best.

Conclusion

By introducing tawakkul to children in simple, engaging ways, you help them develop a strong sense of trust in Allah from an early age. Through stories, activities, and daily practices, children learn that while they must put in effort, it is Allah who ultimately controls the outcome. As they grow, this foundational understanding of tawakkul will help them face life's challenges with faith, resilience, and confidence in Allah's plan.

"The key to contentment lies in knowing that our role is to try, but the result is always in Allah's hands."

## Chapter 8: Exercises to Strengthen Your Trust in Allah

Tawakkul, or trust in Allah, is a deeply spiritual practice that requires both faith and conscious effort. Strengthening tawakkul is not something that happens overnight; it is a journey of reflection, practice, and devotion. In this chapter, we will explore various practical exercises designed to help you develop and deepen your trust in Allah. These exercises are meant to be integrated into your daily life, helping you cultivate reliance on Allah in everything you do.

### 8.1 Exercise 1: The Dua of Tawakkul

Making dua (supplication) is one of the most powerful ways to connect with Allah and express your trust in Him. By regularly making dua and asking Allah for help, guidance, and strength, you solidify your relationship with Him and acknowledge that He is the ultimate source of all outcomes.

Steps to Perform:

1. Choose a Daily Time for Dua: Set aside time each day for a few minutes of heartfelt dua. You can do this after salah (prayer), before bed, or at any quiet moment. Consistency is key.
2. Make Dua for Specific Needs: During your dua, ask Allah for help in a specific matter. Whether you are facing a personal challenge, need guidance, or seek protection from harm, bring these matters to Allah. Express your trust that He will take care of it in the best possible way.
3. Recite a Dua for Tawakkul: There are specific duas that emphasize reliance on Allah. One of the most powerful is:

"Hasbiyallahu la ilaha illa Huwa, 'alayhi tawakkaltu wa Huwa Rabbul 'Arshil 'Azim."
Translation: "Allah is sufficient for me; there is no deity except Him. I have placed my trust in Him, and He is the Lord of the mighty Throne."
(Surah At-Tawbah 9:129)

4. Conclude with Gratitude: End your dua by thanking Allah for everything He has given you, and affirm that you trust His wisdom in all outcomes.

Reflection: After a few weeks of consistent dua, reflect on how this practice has impacted your sense of reliance on Allah. Do you feel more peaceful or confident about the matters you've entrusted to Him?

Exercise 2: **Trust in Allah Visualization Exercise**

This visualization exercise helps you mentally and emotionally internalize the concept of Tawakkul, especially when facing uncertainty.

Steps:

1. Find a Quiet Space: Sit in a quiet place where you won't be disturbed. Close your eyes and take deep breaths to calm yourself.
2. Visualize Your Challenge: Imagine a situation in your life where you feel uncertainty or fear. Visualize it clearly in your mind.
3. Surrender to Allah: Picture yourself handing over that situation to Allah, much like physically placing it in His hands. Imagine the weight lifting off your shoulders as you say to yourself, "I trust in Allah's wisdom."
4. Affirm Trust: Repeat the affirmation: "I trust Allah to guide me, no matter what happens."

Reflection: After the visualization, reflect on how you feel. Did visualizing the process of surrendering your challenge to Allah bring peace? How can you maintain that trust throughout the day?

### Exercise 3: **The Surrender Box Exercise**

This physical exercise helps you develop the habit of surrendering control and trusting in Allah by symbolically "letting go" of your worries.

Steps:

1. Create a Surrender Box: Find a small box and label it your "Surrender Box." This box represents handing over your worries and concerns to Allah.
2. Write Your Worries: Each time you feel anxious about something, write it down on a small piece of paper. Fold it and place it in the box, symbolizing your act of trust and surrender to Allah.
3. Make a Dua: As you place the paper in the box, make a dua asking Allah to take care of the matter and help you trust His outcome.
4. Review Periodically: At the end of each month, open the box and review the concerns you wrote down. Reflect on how Allah has addressed these concerns, either by resolving them or helping you grow through them.

Reflection: This exercise provides a tangible reminder of your decision to trust Allah. Reflect on how it feels to release control over these matters.

### Exercise 4: **Morning Tawakkul Affirmation**

This exercise helps you start your day by affirming your trust in Allah, creating a mindset of reliance on Him before the day's challenges even begin.

Steps:

1. **Choose an Affirmation:** Select an affirmation that resonates with you, such as:
   - "Today, I trust Allah's plan and know that everything will unfold in the best way."
   - "I rely on Allah's wisdom, and I know that whatever comes my way is for my ultimate good."
2. **Repeat the Affirmation:** As soon as you wake up, before starting any tasks, repeat the affirmation aloud or in your mind at least five times.
3. **Set Your Intention:** Mentally set an intention for the day that aligns with trust. For example, "I will work hard and leave the results to Allah," or "I will be patient and trust that Allah is guiding me in every step."

Reflection: After a week of practicing this morning routine, reflect on how it has affected your sense of trust throughout the day. Are you less anxious? Are you handling challenges with more calm and faith?

### Exercise 5: **Salah of Tawakkul (Prayer of Trust)**

This exercise combines a special prayer and reflection to help reinforce your Tawakkul through regular spiritual practice.

Steps:

1. **Perform Two Rakat of Salah:** Set aside a special time to perform two rakat of prayer, intending to increase your trust in Allah.
2. **Make a Specific Dua:** After completing the prayer, raise your hands and make dua, asking Allah to help you trust Him more deeply in all aspects of your life.
3. **Reflect on Surrender:** As you finish the prayer, sit in quiet reflection. Ask yourself: Have I done my part in this matter? What more can I leave in Allah's hands?

Reflection: Journaling after this practice can help. Write down what you feel you've surrendered to Allah and any insights you gained about trust during the prayer.

"Tawakkul is the heart's compass, guiding us through life's uncertainties with faith in Allah's plan."

## Chapter 9: Overcoming Doubts and Challenges with Tawakkul

In this chapter, we will explore how Tawakkul (trust in Allah) can be a guiding principle to overcome doubts, fears, and the inevitable challenges we face in life. While doubts are a natural part of human experience, Tawakkul serves as a powerful antidote to uncertainty, providing a sense of peace and assurance that everything is unfolding according to Allah's perfect plan. This chapter will cover:

- The nature of doubts and how they manifest in the lives of believers.
- The importance of understanding that doubts are not necessarily a sign of weak faith, but an opportunity for spiritual growth.
- How Tawakkul strengthens faith and helps believers navigate trials with patience, resilience, and peace of mind.

### 9.1 Understanding the Nature of Doubts

Every believer at some point may face doubts—whether about personal choices, relationships, or even religious faith itself. It's essential to recognize that doubts are a natural part of life, especially when faced with uncertainty or hardship. Doubts often stem from:

- **Fear of the Unknown:** When the future is unclear, people often feel anxious and uncertain about what will happen next.
- **Difficult Life Situations:** Financial struggles, health crises, and family issues can shake even the strongest faith.
- **Pressure from Society:** Constant comparisons with others or societal pressures can lead to doubts about self-worth or one's path in life.

- Lack of Immediate Results: When prayers go unanswered or success seems delayed, doubts about Allah's plan may begin to surface.

These doubts can weaken a person's sense of direction, leading to stress, worry, and even spiritual crisis. However, instead of letting doubts consume you, you can see them as a call to strengthen your Tawakkul.

9.2 How Tawakkul Overcomes Doubts

Tawakkul is about trusting Allah's wisdom and mercy, knowing that whatever happens is part of His greater plan. It provides the spiritual resilience to push through moments of doubt by reminding believers that:

- Allah is in Control: No matter how uncertain or challenging a situation may seem, Allah is fully aware of what's happening and is in control of every detail. Trusting in His plan helps you let go of anxiety.
- Trials Have a Purpose: The Qur'an teaches that trials and difficulties are tests of faith and opportunities for growth. Allah states:

  "And We will surely test you with something of fear and hunger and a loss of wealth and lives and fruits, but give good tidings to the patient" (Qur'an 2:155).

- Patience Brings Reward: When doubts arise due to hardships, remember that patience (sabr) paired with Tawakkul leads to immense rewards in both this life and the Hereafter. The believer is not passive, but rather takes action while relying on Allah's plan.

Exercise: Reflect on Your Doubts

1. Write down any doubts or fears that you've recently experienced, whether they relate to your personal life or your faith.

2. Reflect on each doubt and ask yourself: Have I done everything within my power to address this situation? If yes, then why am I still holding onto anxiety?
3. Recite the dua: "Hasbunallahu wa ni'mal wakeel" (Allah is sufficient for us, and He is the best disposer of affairs) and visualize handing over your worry to Allah.

## 9.3 Trusting the Process: Trials as a Path to Growth

Challenges and hardships can often feel like roadblocks, but in the light of Tawakkul, they are seen as pathways to spiritual growth. The Prophet Muhammad (PBUH) himself went through immense challenges—from the loss of loved ones to societal opposition—yet his unwavering trust in Allah allowed him to overcome these trials with grace.

### Case Study: The Prophet Ibrahim's Tawakkul

One of the most powerful examples of Tawakkul in overcoming challenges is the story of Prophet Ibrahim (AS). When he was commanded by Allah to sacrifice his son, Prophet Ibrahim (AS) trusted in Allah's wisdom without question. Though he faced an incredibly difficult test, his Tawakkul led to Allah replacing the sacrifice with a ram, demonstrating that faith and trust bring ultimate relief and divine reward.

This story teaches us that even in moments of extreme uncertainty or difficulty, trusting in Allah's plan is always the best course of action.

## 9.4 Overcoming Fear of the Future with Tawakkul

Fear of the future is a common cause of doubt. People often wonder what will happen next: Will my efforts bear fruit? Will I be successful? Will I be able to handle the challenges ahead? These fears are rooted in the desire for control over outcomes.

Tawakkul helps eliminate the need for absolute control by instilling the belief that:

- **Allah is the Best Planner:** No amount of worrying can change what Allah has decreed, but trusting in His plan brings inner peace. As the Qur'an reminds us:

  "But they plan, and Allah plans. And Allah is the best of planners" (Qur'an 8:30).

- **Sufficient Provision:** Tawakkul teaches that Allah will provide what you need at the right time, even if it differs from your expectations. Trusting in this provision helps release the fear of scarcity or failure.

Exercise: Trust the Future

1. Write down your goals and dreams, both short-term and long-term. Next to each one, write what you can do to achieve them, and what is beyond your control.
2. Acknowledge what you can control, and then mentally surrender the rest to Allah's wisdom.
3. Say the prayer of contentment: "O Allah, I entrust my affairs to You and am content with Your plan for me."

## 9.5 Letting Go of the Need for Immediate Results

In a world driven by instant gratification, it's easy to lose patience when things don't happen as quickly as we expect. However, Tawakkul helps ease the frustration that comes from delayed results. Trust in Allah includes trusting His timing, which is always perfect, even if it doesn't align with our desires.

- **Patience and Trust:** Believing that Allah will provide the right outcome at the right time helps to build patience. As we wait for results, we learn to appreciate the journey, trusting that it is shaping us in ways we may not yet understand.

Exercise: Reflect on Delayed Results

1. Identify a situation in your life where you are waiting for an outcome, such as a job offer, a relationship resolution, or personal progress.

2. Reflect on how this waiting period has taught you patience, faith, or resilience.
3. Ask yourself: How can I continue to trust that Allah's timing is best, even if I don't see immediate results?

## 9.6 Building Resilience through Tawakkul

When you trust in Allah, you naturally build spiritual and emotional resilience. Tawakkul enables you to bounce back from setbacks because you understand that nothing happens without Allah's knowledge and decree. This realization allows you to stay calm and maintain perspective, even in the face of adversity.

Action Steps to Build Resilience:

- Seek Allah's Help First: Before turning to others for advice or comfort, make it a habit to ask Allah for guidance through dua and prayer.
- Reframe Your Setbacks: When faced with a challenge, remind yourself that it is an opportunity to grow closer to Allah. Ask: "What is Allah teaching me through this situation?"
- Develop a Support System: Surround yourself with people who encourage Tawakkul and can remind you of Allah's wisdom when you feel overwhelmed.

## 9.7 Practical Ways to Strengthen Tawakkul When Facing Doubts

- Increase Dhikr: Repeating phrases like "La hawla wa la quwwata illa billah" (There is no power and no strength except with Allah) strengthens the heart and reminds you that all power belongs to Allah alone.
- Consult the Qur'an and Hadith: When doubts arise, turn to the words of Allah and the teachings of the Prophet Muhammad (PBUH) for guidance and reassurance.
- Perform Salat al-Istikhara: This special prayer is a means of asking for Allah's guidance in making decisions, reinforcing that we trust Him to guide us toward the best outcome.

Exercise: Tawakkul Diary

1. Over the course of a month, keep a diary of moments when you feel doubt or fear. Write down how you responded—did you rely on yourself or trust in Allah?
2. Track any prayers, dhikr, or actions you took to remind yourself of Tawakkul.
3. At the end of the month, review your entries and reflect on how your trust in Allah has grown. How has your response to doubt changed?


Conclusion

Tawakkul serves as a powerful tool to overcome doubts, fears, and uncertainties. By relying on Allah, believers can transform challenges into opportunities for growth and spiritual refinement. As we trust in Allah's wisdom and timing, we learn to let go of our need for control and instead embrace the peace that comes from knowing that everything is unfolding according to a divine plan.

## Conclusion: Living a Life Anchored in Trust

As we reach the conclusion of this book on Tawakkul, it's clear that living a life anchored in trust in Allah brings unparalleled peace, resilience, and fulfillment. Tawakkul is more than just a passive acceptance of fate; it's an active and conscious effort to align our hearts with the certainty that Allah is the ultimate planner. Trusting Him, we are free from the burden of trying to control every outcome, knowing that Allah's wisdom is far greater than our understanding.

In this journey, we've explored various dimensions of Tawakkul, from understanding its deep theological roots to applying it in practical, everyday scenarios. Whether facing doubts, struggles, or uncertainty, Tawakkul guides us to a place of patience, serenity, and spiritual clarity. It transforms how we approach life's challenges, strengthens our connection with Allah, and elevates our inner peace.

Key Lessons Recapped:

1. Tawakkul is an Active Trust: It's not about abandoning effort or resigning ourselves to fate. Instead, Tawakkul teaches us to take responsible action while leaving the results in Allah's hands. As Prophet Muhammad (PBUH) taught, "Tie your camel, then trust in Allah."
2. Faith Over Fear: In a world full of uncertainties, Tawakkul helps us replace fear with faith. The more we trust Allah, the less room there is for anxiety or fear of the unknown.
3. Patience and Gratitude: Trusting Allah involves being patient during trials and being grateful for whatever outcome He decrees. Patience (sabr) and gratitude (shukr) are key pillars of a trusting heart.
4. Strength in Struggles: We learned through stories of the Prophets and other examples that trials are part of life, but they are opportunities to strengthen our reliance on Allah. The greater the struggle, the more our Tawakkul deepens.

5. Practical Application: From daily dhikr to reflecting on Allah's wisdom, there are numerous ways to practice and strengthen Tawakkul. Exercises such as journaling, making dua, and using specific prayers like Salat al-Istikhara help keep us anchored in trust.

A Life of Serenity Through Tawakkul

When you live with Tawakkul, life's burdens become lighter. You realize that you are not responsible for controlling every detail of your life, and this realization brings peace. You work hard, pursue your goals, and make plans, but you rest in the certainty that Allah's plan is always perfect, even when it's different from what you had hoped.

As you navigate through life's ups and downs, Tawakkul allows you to experience tranquility in the midst of chaos. It doesn't mean life will be free from hardship, but it does mean that you'll face every challenge with a heart anchored in trust. You'll stop worrying about the "what ifs" and instead focus on what you can control—your efforts, your intentions, and your trust in Allah.

A Call to Action: Strengthen Your Trust

As you move forward, continue to cultivate Tawakkul in your life. Make it a daily practice, especially in moments of doubt or anxiety. Remember, trust in Allah is not a one-time achievement; it's a lifelong journey. The more you practice it, the more natural it will become.

- Reflect Daily: Take time each day to reflect on your actions and intentions. Ask yourself if you truly trust Allah with your affairs, or if you're holding onto control.
- Use Dua as a Tool: Whenever you feel overwhelmed, turn to dua. Ask Allah for the strength to trust Him and surrender your worries.

- Practice Gratitude: Even when things don't go as planned, practice gratitude. Remember that Allah's wisdom is always greater than our understanding.
- Teach Others: Share the lessons of Tawakkul with your family, friends, and community. Help others cultivate this life-transforming trust in Allah.

Tawakkul: The Ultimate Source of Inner Peace

As we conclude this journey, know that Tawakkul is a powerful force for inner peace. It is the essence of faith, the heart of worship, and the key to living a balanced, resilient life. By anchoring ourselves in Tawakkul, we fulfill our purpose as believers—to trust in Allah wholeheartedly and live according to His will.

May Allah (SWT) grant us all the strength to develop unwavering trust in Him. May He guide us through our doubts, fears, and challenges, and may we always find peace in knowing that our affairs rest in His perfect wisdom.

Ameen.

"Tawakkul is trusting that what is meant for you will never miss you, and what misses you was never meant for you." – Jamshed Durrani

The Islamic Mindset Series:

www.catalysticcoach.com

Printed in Great Britain
by Amazon